Guru

BY FIXING ONLY ONE PIECE
OF THE JIGSAW PUZZLE,

YOU'LL MISS SEEING
THE WHOLE PICTURE.

Guru

RUPAUL

FOREWORD BY JANE FONDA

DEY ST.

An Imprint of WILLIAM MORROW

DEY ST.

HarperCollins books may be purchased for educational, business, or sales promotional use. For information, please email the Special Markets Department at SPsales@harpercollins.com.

FIRST EDITION

Designed by Suet Yee Chong

Library of Congress Cataloging-in-Publication Data has been applied for.

ISBN 978-0-06-286299-0

18 19 20 21 22   LSC   10 9 8 7 6 5 4 3 2 1

To all you sweet, sensitive souls out there in the world—
look for the light in the world, in people, in places,
in art and music. Light will lift you up.

CONTENTS

FOREWORD

by Jane Fonda

I was so honored when my friend RuPaul Charles asked me to write a few words for his new book, *GuRu*, which you now have in your hands. Like you, I have witnessed all the beauty and power that is RuPaul. But I have been lucky enough to experience this in person—most recently when Ru asked me to present him with his star on the Hollywood Walk of Fame earlier this year. That was a very special day—for both of us. RuPaul reminded me that seeing me as Barbarella on the cover of *Life* magazine had been an early inspiration for him. I was touched, as one always is when you hear that you've inspired someone. But it is truly wonderful when the person you inspired is someone who has inspired so many themselves.

RuPaul has touched millions in his three decades in the public eye. He has done this by being who he really is, but finding the best and most powerful version of that person was a journey. In this book, RuPaul presents parts of his journey in words and photographs. Here he tells you what he thinks about his craft, his past, his loved ones, his team, meditation, and how to work through darkness and find the light. With depth, intelligence, and always humor,

RuPaul shares the gift of himself in the pages of this book, just as he does on the set of his groundbreaking show, on his podcast, and in all of his work and life. As I said in my introduction of him at the Hollywood Walk of Fame, his star should be three times larger than the rest. I say that because I truly believe that RuPaul's heart and his accomplishments are three times larger than almost anyone's I know. It is a pleasure to know him, and *GuRu* is a pleasure to read. I hope you will enjoy it as much as I do.

everybody say love

Welcome to the house of Mama Ru, my beautiful child. Here, we will explore the path of the seeker. The one who dares to feel more, to experience more, and to fearlessly love more. Together, we will uncover ancient sacred "realness" that is tried, tested, and found true. I will share everything I've learned from the journey thus far; my only wish is that you pass the knowledge along to the next traveler, even if that traveler is me. *GuRu* is a collection of mantras, sayings, and touchstones that I've used throughout this surreal daydream of a life to remind me of who I really am. I am a shapeshifter whose only mission is to experience humanity. It's as simple as that, but as questions arise, the need to go deeper beckons. I continue to walk through my fears, superstitions, and self-imposed limitations, some with more trepidation than others, but still I keep on walking. Think of *GuRu* as an additional GPS to be used in support of your own built-in navigation system. How does "drag" factor into all of this? Well, I'm sure you've heard me say, "You're born naked and the rest is drag." In truth, you are not your clothes, you are not your profession, you are not your religion. You are an extension of the consciousness that guides the universe, for which there is no name because it cannot be defined. That's why all the superficial things you list as your identity are in reality your "drag." Years ago, when I heard someone say "we are all God in drag," I knew it to be the true at my core.

Just know that by stepping through this door, a lot of things you thought to be "real" will be challenged. Basically, prepare for your mind to be blown. Not to worry though, kiddo. This is the new normal for the seeker. Budget in plenty of occasions for the death and rebirth of ideas and concepts.

Drag is the highest form of being, of showing our best selves to the world.

But we have to learn how to love ourselves, and there are a lot of you out there who need some lessons on how to do just that. I say "love yourself" all the time, but knowing how to go about it can be a mystery. Now, listen to me. It's still an ongoing process for me. The key is to remember to keep yourself up and to keep on walking. Don't worry about what lies ahead, or if you're being judged by other people. Use the frequency as your guide.

I'm a living witness to the revelation that once you get rid of all the negativity in your world, everything and everyone that might be blocking you, you will live in the light. Inside of us all is great power, creativity, and beauty. Your saboteurs may have all that same creativity and power, too, and they may trick you into believing that you aren't worth your value. But when I look out at the world, when I meet my fans, what I see is pure love and gorgeousness. So, what I hope that GuRu will do for you is help you see your own love and gorgeousness, too, and shut out the negativity and naysayers once and for all.

When I was a kid my mother and father divorced, and my father was supposed to come and pick my sisters and me up on the weekends. There we would be, my sisters and I, sitting on that porch waiting for him. And he would not show up. We were the most beautiful kids you'd ever want to see. We really were gorgeous. And all of my time in therapy in the years since then were spent making peace with that moment when my father didn't appear, when he left us sitting there on that porch waiting for him. Time and time again I have recreated that victimhood in my life, in love, in all kinds of storylines that made me feel the way I felt as an abandoned child. For years, I built my identity around that little boy who was left behind. I didn't treat myself very kindly, either, because if I was a boy who could be left behind, then why love myself, or honor my body like a temple? I had to learn to let go of that boy so I could start to love.

I like to think of my body as my vehicle, my human machine. At this point, I have put a lot of miles on my vehicle. And sometimes, the wheel likes to turn a little bit to the left when it's raining. Your body knows when there's a storm a-brewing, when the vehicle needs a tune-up, and you can take that concept and apply it to every aspect of your life.

When I wake up in the morning, the first thing I do is stretch, because I'm getting older and this body needs to be stretched. But after that, I get down on my knees and I pray. I pray every single morning. My prayer is very simple, but it is very powerful. It goes like this:

"Dear God [that's what I say, and you can use whatever you choose], I thank you. I ask that you guide my thoughts, my feelings, and my perceptions. I willingly give you all of my resentments."

The act of prayer provides the human machine a method for rigging the system. We can't see ourselves, really, and spiritual practices help us remember that something else is running this whole thing. Prayer, getting down on your knees and deactivating that ego, is acknowledging that there's a presence greater than myself. It circumvents the whole system and allows for a special intervention between me and something bigger. The ego is completely silent when I am bowing down. After I pray, I meditate. Meditation is like watching a river flowing while you are sitting on the bank. The water is your consciousness. You can watch your thoughts pass by without judgment, allowing your body to become a transmitter, a channeling system. It doesn't matter how long you do it—two minutes, thirty seconds, twenty minutes—the practice turns your body into a transmitter for a signal that magic can happen.

The acts of meditation and of prayer are the practices that help me reset the machine, shut down the ego, and love myself.

If I had stayed in the mentality of that little boy who was left behind on that porch, I wouldn't be who I am today. I wouldn't be doing the things I do, creating the art and living the life I have. I wouldn't have found the love I have with my husband, Georges, because I would still be so blocked that I would be getting in my own way constantly. We all have angels around us who want to help, but because we have free will they cannot intervene unless we say three little words: "Please help me." You just have to be brave enough and self-aware enough and love yourself enough to ask. Clear out the blockage that keeps you playing small, keeps you listening to the negative stories in your head, keeps you in the darkness, and move forward into the light. You have the power to move on if you're willing to let go of the limited perception you have of yourself. You are God's gift to this world and you are the manifestation of the power that created the whole universe.

The universe always has stage directions for you if you're open, if you clear a place for it. With *GuRu*, I challenge each of you to do a diagnostic test on your human machine. Take an objective view and ask, "Where are the places I am stuck?" Use this book as a tool along your journey to discovering that it is no accident that you are here to experience life and humanity, and that is the joy of life. I realized that I didn't come to this planet in this beautiful body to live this beautiful life to be asleep during the whole process. I have become a seeker, and I know all of you are seekers, too. Find the life you want. Find all that life has to offer. Hopefully, what you find here will inspire you, entertain you, and remind you not to take yourself, or anything for that matter, too seriously. That is what loving yourself is.

Oh, and remember, Mama Ru loves you.

Every twenty-eight years, Saturn returns to the same position where it was at your birth and presents you with challenges. My first Saturn return was horrific, humiliating, and soul-crushing, but very valuable, because when it was over, I realized I had developed an emotional musculature that was tough as steel. I had learned to dig my feet into the ground as the storm passed over me. And in the end, I had real strength and fortitude, and truly understood my own personal resilience. Now, twenty-eight years later, Saturn returns again. Though less traumatic, this time it's about clearing up unfinished business. Now I'm willing to be emotionally naked, and feel confident in the power that comes from just being me. I feel unafraid to reveal myself, a new level of me. It was exhausting making sure other people were okay with me. Chile, ain't nobody got time for that! If my outlook and ambition are intimidating to people, so be it. In the past, drag has stealthily allowed my true self to fly under the radar. Revealing all of the unfiltered parts of me is where I am now.

Getting ready to go onstage or in front of the cameras is like preparing for battle. When I get all dolled up to film *Drag Race*, I'll take six hours. I could do it in two hours, but it's important for me to make it a deliberately sacred, drawn-out ritual. I have separate rooms for costumes, hair, makeup, and lounging, and even a room for podcasting. The people who help me get ready—"the magic team"—are all filled with the same creative warrior spirit. We know the world is watching, so we want to give them something special. I thrive in a creative atmosphere. That's why if one of us is not 100 percent, we all have to pitch in and lift the other one up. When I'm alone, I've learned to replenish that energy through prayer, meditation, and stillness. Being fully present in the moment will also get you energy.

IF YOU WANT TO
BE INVITED TO THE
PARTY, YOU MUST HAVE
SOMETHING TO BRING.

Seeing myself transformed is such a trip. I've never gotten used to seeing myself in drag. Or out of drag for that matter. I've always felt like The Boy Who Fell to Earth and landed in this body. I want to do as much as I can with this body while I have it. It's all about honoring this beautiful, gorgeous gift, painting it and decorating it. Why not put on your best every day? Put your best foot forward. Even if it's just for yourself, even if it is for a trip to the grocery store or to the dry cleaners—why not put on your best?

Never pass up an opportunity to wear a fancy outfit, even if you're the only one who appreciates it.

I bow down to anyone who will wear a false eyelash between the hours of 9 A.M. and 5 P.M. I bow at their feet, because it is a true commitment to Glamazon. And of course, extra points for lower lashes.

Glamazon defined.

I am truly an introvert masquerading as an extrovert. The Scorpio in me can be very intense for most people. Drag has allowed me to lighten up. The same way that most people express another side of themselves when they dress up for Halloween. In between shots, I like to conserve my energy and just save it all for when the cameras are rolling.

#ASKYOURSELF:

WHO AM I, REALLY?

To the human eye, proportions are everything. Most people don't realize just how much they react to proportions. I love nudging proportions. I have very long legs, a short torso, and a short neck. You'll notice that I don't put a lot of jewelry around my neck. I like to keep the neck area open and unobstructed so as to elongate it. You'll also see that I take many photos with my mouth open. To get the right proportion for my face. If I wear my hair flat, there is still height at the crown of the head, which elongates everything above the shoulders. It's all about nudging those proportions to get it right, based on how the human eye perceives silhouettes.

You must be willing to see yourself from outside yourself.

THE UNIVERSE
HAS YOUR STAGE
DIRECTION.
#PAYATTENTION

Throughout my career, I've relied on a handful of people who have always had my best interests at heart. People whom I love and trust. And who can offer me a unique perspective that I can't always see on my own. Finding those people is not easy, especially in show business. The people in this photo are those people for me. The man driving this golf cart is someone I met in 1985 in Times Square at a music convention I was wearing football shoulder pads, a loincloth, and a mohawk. Someone introduced us and in that moment, everything I dreamed was achievable in my career, I saw reflected in his eyes. I could see that he was looking at a superstar. Needless to say, I've been working with Randy Barbato ever since. Stick with the ones who have vision. The ones who can not only dream it, but can also make it happen. Stick with the winners, baby.

From childhood I always felt very unique, yet I could sense that to most people I was invisible. They didn't know which box to put me in, so I think it was easier to just see past me. Back then, in gay male culture, if you didn't fit into any of the porn-informed stereotypes, you were seen as a eunuch whose sole purpose was to serve as an accessory. It wasn't until I got into drag for the first time that people really started to take notice. That first time, and every time since, it felt like Clark Kent turning into Superman. I felt powerful. I felt that people could finally see that I was a force to be reckoned with.

Doing drag change who it actually you are.

doesn't
you are,
reveals who

YOU'RE BORN NAKED

When in doubt, go for a three-quarter pose at the camera. It's an angle that captures the best of the cheekbones, the chin line, and a long neck. A three-quarter pose generally suits most people.

AND THE REST IS SHADING AND CONTOURING.

I've always thought of Halloween as amateur night. Just one day to dress up? REALLY? My philosophy has always been: Why not dress up every day? Even as a kid, I rejected the concept of Halloween for that

---

Don't let the weight of the world flatten your weave.

---

reason. I loved the candy, but hated the idea of just one sanctioned day for "dressing up." As an adult, I dress up every day . . . except on Halloween.

Wow, is that really me? I've never quite gotten used to seeing myself in the mirror, in drag or out of drag. The question "Who am I?" always creates a deafening silence in the soul. I believe the depth of that silence is the answer. Where do *you* begin and end? Who are you? What are you? I still feel like The Boy Who Fell to Earth, fell into this body, and is experiencing humanity, having fun with it.

DON'T BE AFRAID OF YOUR POWER.

I've been shunned by whites for being black, by blacks for being gay, and by gays for being fem. The real tee? The ego needs to feel superior over others. The art of shapeshifting also includes reading the energy in the room. Protect yourself from ignorance and keep out of harm's way. And know that the hurtful things people say have everything to do with them and not you. It is simply an outward projection of their own self-loathing. Bless them. And by all means, don't let your ego co-opt the situation or get involved. Part of your job as a businessperson and diplomat is to get what you need and to not take it too personally.

There's a certain detachment sensitive people must maintain to endure the harsh realities of this world.

Things aren't always as they seem. There are different levels of consciousness. Different vibrations. Drag reminds us that the divisions we create to make sense of what is real and not real are all but our own little superficial illusions. Go with it and get out of the habit of trying to make sense of it all. Practice just being.

A

LITTLE

PERSPECTIVE.

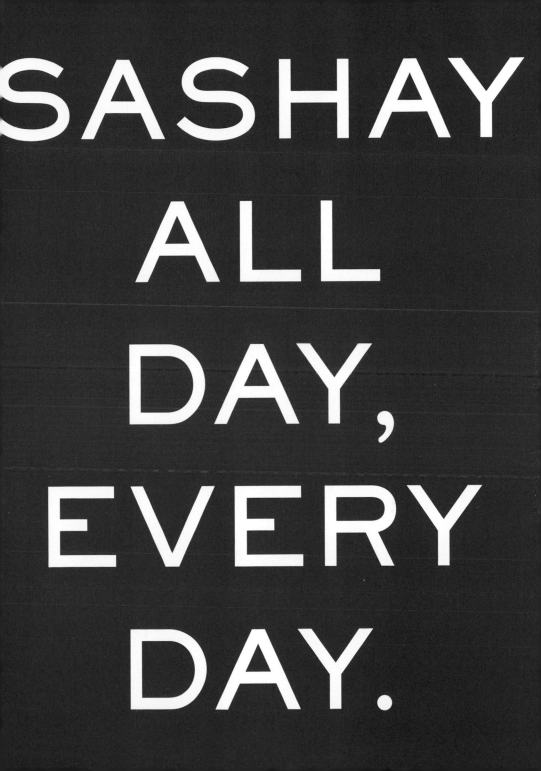

My waist is ridiculously cinched and the butt is padded beyond recognition. All of this is because when wearing a traditionally men's garment in "ladykins" drag, one must overfeminize the body in order to keep the slacks from looking too butch. I mean, come on! A man wearing pants is gonna look totally butch unless you pad that booty to high heaven!

QUICK REMINDER:

HAVING A FAT ASS IS A GOOD THING.

I call my wigs "girls." This girl is probably twenty-five years old and has worked really hard for me over the years. And I've worked hard to keep her in tip-top shape. They all get de-glued, cleaned, and conditioned regularly. Of course, she was born back before the proliferation of all the new machine-made lace-front wigs that you can buy for less than $100. This girl probably paid for my house.

You are cordially invited to Lacefront Manor.

Never underestimate the power of a smoky eye, especially if you are new to makeup and want to do something really dramatic. The first stop for drama is making sure you have on false eyelashes. For next-level drama, go for the smoky eye.

When there are no words, let the eyes do the talking.

Health is wealth. You'll get to a certain age and realize the most valuable currency is good health. Take good care of your body, and be mindful of the thoughts you think. Eventually, all of the thoughts you think will show up on your face. Think healthy thoughts. Even if you have every right to complain, don't do it. If it's raining, learn to dance in the rain. You are the architect of your life. Please believe it and let that be the reason.

YOUR HEALTH IS THE MOST VALUABLE THING YOU HAVE. PROTECT IT.

I've been a daydreamer since day one. I much prefer looking out a window over looking at my phone.

MY LIPS ARE OVERDRAWN TO COMPENSATE FOR MY LACK OF GIVING A SHIT.

I've heard that laughter is the most powerful spell you can cast. I'd also say that a beautiful smile is right up there, too. During my twenties I didn't take good care of my teeth, and paid dearly for it in my forties. The ones in front are my natural teeth, but all the ones in back are implants. At the very least, floss and brush in the morning and at night. Also, a water irrigator used with mouthwash will save you a lot of misery later.

AVOID DUMB PEOPLE. DO NOT TRY TO EDUCATE THEM OR TRY TO PROVE HOW SUPERIOR YOU ARE TO THEM. JUST SMILE AND STAY AWAY FROM THEM.

I've always loved pop culture. Irreverent pop art. The Warhol aesthetic. Magazines, album covers. Fashion. David Bowie. My mind cataloged the imagery, the shapes and silhouettes. It's great to work with people who also know those references, because it's a shortcut to the creative process. In fact, I prefer working with people who have that vernacular and who know the references— in songwriting, moviemaking, television, design. I'm worried that young people don't have enough curators and mentors needed to learn this language.

First learn the rules, then break them.

The color red always gets me excited. Blood red makes me feel dangerous and in the moment. Explore all the colors to see what effect they have on your energy. Use them on yourself as a conductor would command an orchestra!

USE ALL THE COLORS IN THE CRAYON BOX.

CONSCIOUSNESS
IS SO
sexy.

My drag look has had several incarnations, but the one that became my signature look was conceived by the marketing man in
me. I wanted a recognizable silhouette that could be easily drawn
by a caricature artist and emulated by a sketch comedy troupe. I
started this process by borrowing liberally from the pop stars I
admired. I took two parts Diana Ross, one part David Bowie, three
parts Cher, and a heaping spoonful of Dolly Parton. All of those
elements together created the look that made me an international
star. I call it Glamazon.

GENIUS: 1 PERCENT INSPIRATION + 99 PERCENT FULL-COVERAGE FOUNDATION.

I've always loved beautiful clothes, men's or women's, it doesn't matter. Just as long as they're beautiful. I adore different textures and colors. Shiny Mylar, heavy tweeds, bold prints; I love them all! Children are inherently drawn to those things, and I never lost that. My older sister reminds me all the time that I was running around the backyard in her clothes as soon as I could walk. I wasn't thinking "this is drag," I was thinking "this is fun." For me the fun never stopped. And why should it? My first deliberately drag look was called "gender f%k." I was part of the Atlanta bohemian/punk rock scene. We wore combat boots, torn dresses, and smeared lipstick. All while flipping the bird. When I moved to New York City, I needed to make money, so I took a job as a go-go dancer on the bar at the Pyramid Club. I decided to switch my look to something more approachable and tip-inducing. I chose a look somewhere between streetwalker and *Soul Train* dancer. Needless to say, I was a big hit.

Before settling on the Glamazon, my drag aesthetic was streetwalker/ Soul Train dancer . . . still my favorite look.

I've always been fascinated by space exploration. Stanley Kubrick's *2001: A Space Odyssey* totally blew my mind. It opened up doorways in my consciousness that have never been closed again. The concept of other worlds is so freeing to me. Every morning I awake at four a.m. to stretch, pray, and meditate. I can see the stars from the large sliding glass door in my bedroom. I imagine being out in space looking back at Earth. This tiny blue dot looks so peaceful from there. And all of my perceived problems don't even exist.

"When your eyeliner is on point, your life is on point."

—MEAN MS. CHARLES

At ten years old, I was told by my mother, "Moisturize, moisturize, moisturize!" and I have ever since. Luckily, my skin has been pretty resilient given the amount of makeup and sun I've forced it to endure.

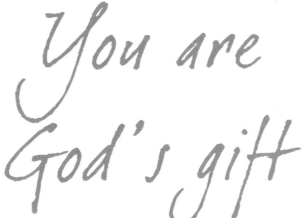

Quick Reminder: You are God's gift to the world.

I don't remember any happy childhood Christmas memories. We were poor and the holidays seemed to only emphasize what our fractured family didn't have. As an adult, I've redefined what Christmas means to me. I take the time to reflect on the past year and focus on gratitude. I love the music and parties, but I don't give gifts because it feels too forced. I will give gifts all year round, just not at Christmas. I also prefer to be someplace warm during the holidays. I have friends who visit family in Buffalo, New York, during the holidays when the temperature is ridiculously cold. I suggested that they call a family meeting to move their holiday festivities to springtime.

QUICK REMINDER: INSTEAD OF CONSTANTLY POINTING OUT WHAT'S MISSING, CELEBRATE WHAT IS.

I learned early on that if I was embarrassed by something, it was definitely something I needed to do. I needed to challenge myself in every single way I possibly could and take it as far as I possibly could. But you have to walk those hard yards. You have to do it to get to the other side; there is no way around it. Challenge yourself to the limits of your fears. Get moving on.

looking stupid

is holding you back.

Punk rock is more than just a style of music, it's an attitude toward life. It's a way of thinking that challenges the status quo and imagines a life outside of society's box. I've spent my life creating my own value system that has little to do with the value system of my parents. Of course, kindness is number one. Being loving is always at the top of my list. But if I tried to fit my worth into what I was taught by society, I'd be worthless. I had to learn what my true value was by forging ahead into the wild frontier. I wanted to be free. And I've done that. But there's a price you pay. You have to find a tribe. And if you don't find a tribe, you're very alone. And there have been many times when I've been alone in my journey. You have to be able to sustain yourself if you don't have other people, because your family may not understand it. Some friends won't even understand it. It does take a strong person to truly be free.

Life is too short with what other

"Breaking the fourth wall" is a theatrical term used to describe when the stage actor acknowledges the audience, thus recognizing that they are playing a role. I've always maintained that we are all actors on a stage and that we play these roles we inherit from society. But if you're able to see that and recognize that it's all an illusion, you have the upper hand in creating where your character can go. If you're able to press the pause button on your life and go outside of yourself and see all the characters you're playing, the dynamics of the scenes, flip forward and back a few pages in the script to see what your character's purpose to the story as a whole is, then you can dictate where you want your character to go. Of course, I am speaking in metaphor here. I always say that it's important to not take life too seriously. Well, that is part of this philosophy of being able to see yourself as a character and to laugh, cry, and make your life an Academy Award-winning performance, because it is all performance.

Seeing yourself from outside yourself allows you to navigate your life and change the course of humanity.

DOLLY PARTON
IS FAMOUS
FOR SAYING,
"NEVER
PERM YOUR
OWN HAIR."
I THINK THAT'S
SOUND ADVICE.

Arriving early is not against the law.

I like to arrive early. If you really want to throw bitches off their game, arrive early. I used to arrive late all the time until I realized I was addicted to the adrenaline rush I got *from being late.* When I was willing to let go of my addiction to the adrenaline, I was able to arrive early. Adrenaline was the payoff, and humans are always looking for a payoff. We do nothing unless there's a payoff. Follow the money. Find the payoff.

Your lighting is important. Light is everything. It's how we see. I have an addiction to buying flashlights. I can't tell you how many I have. The metaphor isn't lost on me. I'm a seeker and I'm always looking for something, trying to see things. I spent

When driving in the rain, always turn on your headlights.

time in darkness. I've spent time in light. I prefer the light. It's important that I did the darkness, it was an experience for me, but if I have a choice, it will always be the light.

PRO TIP:

Keep your neck and bosom area unobstructed to give the appearance of a longer neck.

I just had my condo in New York redone by the man who is the set decorator on *Drag Race*. He makes everything look really gorgeous, but I wanted him to fill the bathroom with mirrors and make it very, very bright. You need that light if you are going to be preparing to spend your day out among people. I want my bathroom to look like an operating room.

Always arrive camera-ready.

On social media I get a lot of people writing to me saying, "Why won't you notice me?" I wanna write them back and say, "Me noticing you will never satisfy your deep craving unless you notice you first." But I won't write that, because most people cannot really hear that simple truth. What people are subconsciously asking is for proof that they actually exist. We all want validation, proof of life, but it must come from you. From the inside out, rather than the outside in.

People are looking to fill that void with some outside source, but that empty feeling can only be filled from within.

This is a pose I perfected at seven years of age. It was lifted directly from the fashion magazines I was obsessed with as a child. It looks like I'm standing on a box. I'm not. I have very, very tall shoes

Don't leave the amusement park without riding all the rides.

on, and I have very, very long legs. And, of course, this dress is beyond, beyond. I wore it on television once, so could never wear this again. It lives in a box in storage, and of course on these pages. One day I'll do a retrospective of all my gowns.

*Dear Joan Crawford,
I ask that you guide
my thoughts,
my feelings, and
my perceptions.*

AMEN.

Joan Crawford is famous for saying, "I never go outside the house unless I look like Joan Crawford the movie star." And the truth is, everyone should have that philosophy, especially in this selfie-obsessed world we live in. Not just to impress other people, but to lift yourself up at all times. People also treat you with more respect when you've taken the time to pull yourself together. Dress well and you'll make more money, too.

I think that the concept of arriving camera-ready is a great metaphor for life. It means that you came to play, seriously. That you made a deliberate effort to suit up and show up for life and everything it has to offer. When you show effort, life will reflect that and give it back to you.

Ultimately, it's about the love you give and the love you allow yourself to receive. Everything else fades away.

THE PHRASE "PLEASE REFRAIN FROM" SHOULD BE FOREVER REPLACED WITH "BITCH, PLEASE!"

Catching a cold is your body's way of saying, "Bitch, you need to sit yo' ass down."

You have to listen to your body's inner dialogue, and there are times, if you're conscious, where your body says, "I feel really good" or "I feel a little run down. I don't feel completely myself." So those are the times you need to sit still and listen. We need to be still, like the big beautiful oak tree that stands resilient, storm after storm, season after season, unchanged in its foundation.

You know, in nature, if you don't evolve you will be phased out. It is that simple. If you don't serve the greater good, if you don't make yourself useful and give the world something it needs, you will become redundant. What used to be a local experience is now accessible globally and we must acknowledge that and act on it. That's why it's important to challenge yourself and try new things.

I CHALLENGE YOU TO STEP OUTSIDE YOUR COMFORT ZONE TODAY.

Try a look from a different era. Late-1960s glam is one of my favorites. It involves big hair, top and lower spider lashes, and frosted lipstick. I draw inspiration here from the film *Valley of the Dolls*, a marvelous camp classic based on the book of the same name by Jacqueline Susann.

EASY FALSE EYELASHES:

CURL AND MASCARA REAL LASHES. CUT FALSE EYELASH STRIP INTO THREE PIECES. WITH TWEEZERS, DIP FAKE LASH PIECES INTO GLUE AND PLACE ON TOP OF REAL LASHES. *Voilà!*

People who are quick to point out the bitchiness of drag queens have probably never spent time with straight guys on the basketball court. Straight guys can be super bitchy! In fact, that's what kept me away from playing more sports. They were just so mean and hurtful I just couldn't take it. And I was good at basketball. It just wasn't enjoyable enough for me to continue playing, with all the animosity.

Mama said, "Ru, you're too GD sensitive."

She was right.

There's not enough dancing in the world. And the fact that there are no daytime discos right now is indicative of the trouble we're in as a society.

Gotta remind yourself to have more fun. Play, dance, and laugh.

STOP TRYING TO FIT IN WHEN YOU WERE **BORN TO STAND OUT.**

Never save bath bombs for later. Never wait for a special occasion to light candles. Don't wait to book a massage. Treat yourself to a spa day. Get yourself a colonic immediately. Now is the time. Your body is a temple. Serve it and it will serve you well.

Folks gon' talk sh*t about you anyway, so you might as well just go ahead and do your own thang.

My drag is less about looking like a woman and more about saying F.U. to the cult of systematic masculinity I was bombarded with as a little boy. As boys, we were taught to fit our emotions into this tiny little box, because that somehow makes other people feel more comfortable. But I never wanted to do that. Truth be told, you don't have to. I feel bad for men in our culture. I think we do everyone a disservice by hiding our emotions

AT
FOURTEEN,
I VOWED
TO ALWAYS
LIVE
OUTSIDE
THE MATRIX.

If you are a liar, you naturally assume everyone else

is lying to you. If you are a cheat, you assume that

everyone is cheating you. If you are kindhearted

You are heir
to the laws of the world
you identify with.

---

and loving, you naturally assume everyone is kind-

hearted and loving toward you. Your experience

here is a reflection of your outward projection.

I have days when I think to myself, "You know, I'm gonna give everyone a break today." You should try it sometime. Have a "Give Bitches a Break" day. I recommend it because you never know when you might be the one who needs that break, you know?

"THE HIGHEST FORM OF WISDOM IS KINDNESS."

—THE TALMUD

TODAY'S

EYEBROW:

STRONG

AND

DETERMINED,

YET OPEN

AND

APPROACHABLE.

Being from San Diego, I've always loved sunbathing. When I turned forty-five, I decided it was time for me to stop doing so much of it. Now I'll lay out by the pool for thirty minutes, and then use a self-tanner for that extra warmth of color to my skin. When applying, just remember to use rubber gloves so that your hands don't get too stained.

Be the star that you are. Shine, baby, shine!

Even as a kid, I had no problem walking in high heels. It just came naturally to me. But here's a bit of advice for those of you who are not so lucky:

If you're going to a wedding, or some other long, drawn-out event and you aren't used to wearing high heels, it's important to remember that closed toes and closed heel pumps are not your friend. Your best bet is a pair of slide-in mules that have an expandable vinyl strap at the low vamp.

I made my entrance in the film *To Wong Foo, Thanks for Everything! Julie Newmar*, feet first, so I decided to wear a pair of six-inch sandals that had several straps crisscrossing my feet. It only took an hour of standing around, take after take, for those straps to feel like razor blades. Now, when you see the movie, you'll realize that my feet aren't showing because they used a close-up shot. I'd worn those shoes for nothing. Oh, well, I was new to moviemaking.

ALWAYS WEAR HIGH HEELS, BECAUSE FLATS ARE FOR QUITTERS.

If you stay
ready, you
ain't got
to get
ready.

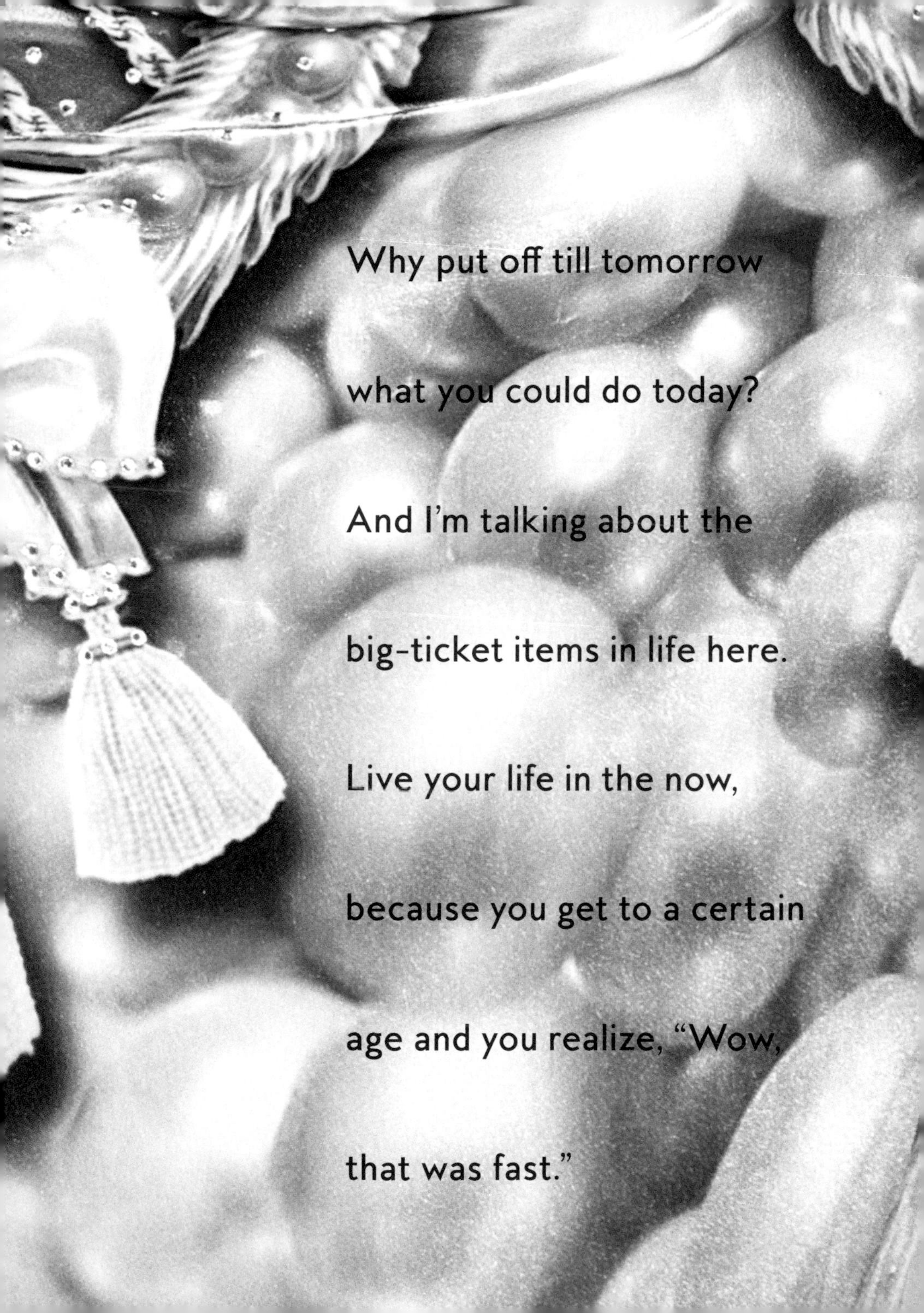

Why put off till tomorrow

what you could do today?

And I'm talking about the

big-ticket items in life here.

Live your life in the now,

because you get to a certain

age and you realize, "Wow,

that was fast."

This outfit was designed and constructed by Bob Mackie. He made it for my Las Vegas show at the Sahara Hotel in 1995. He made all the outfits for that show. I grew up watching *The Carol Burnett Show* and *Sonny and Cher* on TV. So I worshipped

Just because you dreamt it doesn't make it any less real.

at the feet of their costume designer, Bob Mackie. He was clearly influenced by the MGM musicals because his clothes speak to all that color and all that grandeur. I love this outfit. Coincidentally, I was wearing it the first time I met Cher.

My advice is to keep the actual wedding ceremony very small. Go down to City Hall with a handful of people—your parents or closest relatives or even just the two of you. Maybe have the ceremony in your living room with a handful of people. And then, on a separate day, have a great big blowout reception with food and dancing. I think what messes people up is trying to combine the two on the same day. Save yourself the headache of combining two locations and two attitudes into one day.

Keep
an open
heart.

QUICK REMINDER:
Don't dumb down.
Own your greatness.

We often play small, so as not to threaten other people. We don't want to intimidate them by our brightness, but the truth is, you do them and yourself a disservice by dimming what you've been given—your intelligence, your light. Those are your gifts.

Everyone knows about the diminishments of growing older, but no one talks about the expanding strengths. Paired with intellect, your intuition grows increasingly stronger and more on point. Even better is the ability to decipher your sense of knowing. You become a master of reading the room.

How tall?
With hair, heels,
and attitude,
I'm through the
motherf'lokin'
roof.

THROWING SHADE TAKES A BIT OF CREATIVITY. BEING A BITCH TAKES NONE.

All of the artists, performers, and wannabes who had flocked to New York City in my generation had all come to fulfill the Warhol fantasy. We came to claim our fifteen minutes of fame and live like the bohemian rock stars we'd read about in the magazines. I love the Warhol experience. I love the concept of taking a found image and morphing it into another image that speaks to another level

The biggest obstacles I've ever faced were my own self-imposed limitations.

of consciousness. Drag really is all about dipping into pop culture and then reshaping it into something else. And the Warhol experience is really all about that, too. The Warhol Superstars were a bunch of dreamers from the middle of nowhere who came to New York, changed their names, dyed their hair, and became the fabulous concoctions of their own imaginations. And isn't that what we are all doing anyway? Living the dream. If you can dream it, you can be it.

Young people need mentors and curators. The myths of humankind passed along to the next generations. I was lucky enough to have that. People ten years older who showed me the films of Fellini, Antonioni, and Visconti. They gave me the books of Truman Capote and Tennessee Williams, and retold the stories of rebels past.

I barely speak English, but I'm fluent in throwing shade.

I've always been aware that I'm a blessed person. Growing up without a dime to my name, I knew I always had magic. The ability to turn any situation into something special. So if I lost everything tomorrow, I know I'd be just fine. Because here's the thing—having money and fame only enhances what you already are. If you're an asshole before you make money or get famous, you'll be an even bigger asshole after you get rich and famous.

MOST PEOPLE'S
IDEA OF WEALTH
RELIES SOLELY
ON HOW OTHER
PEOPLE SEE THEM.

In most of America, we have massive superstores where you can do everything from buying food, medicine, fresh flowers, and electrical appliances to getting your clothes dry cleaned, all in one location. In New York City, it's very different. You usually have to visit a specific store for each item. Personal relationships are the same way. One person cannot be all things to you like one-stop shopping at a massive superstore. No one wants that kind of pressure or responsibility, and it puts great strain on a relationship. Georges is the great love of my life and my favorite person ever, and he would say the same of me, but we both recognize and acknowledge additional interests outside the universe of two.

"The secret to a happy marriage is separate bedrooms and separate bathrooms."

—BETTE DAVIS

The character I created called Starrbooty was conceived over thirty years ago. Born of my love for the early 1970s genre of film called Blaxploitation, Starrbooty is strong, compassionate, vulnerable, kind, and powerful. I love stories of people who, against all odds, triumph in an unjust world while looking fabulous and kicking serious ass.

AS DRAG QUEENS, IT'S OUR JOB TO MOCK THE HYPOCRISY, MEDIOCRITY, AND ABSURDITY OF SOCIETY.

Before I hit "the big time," I spent my time hanging out with a lot of dreamers. Creative people who would fantasize about what it might be like once the world recognized their unique talent. And talented they were! But most of them didn't have the stamina or the "stickwithitness" it takes to withstand the rejection and humiliation of putting yourself out there to be judged and traded on the open market. Looking back, I guess I didn't know what I was in for either, but in my mind I had no other choice. I was in it for the long haul. After eleven years of "the hard yards" I finally got my big break. I had "made it," but no one warned me that the really hard work was yet to come. The biggest challenge is to maintain it and to stay interested in doing the work. It's very easy to become disillusioned with the business, and hurt by how fickle the audience is. Yes, a support team is essential, but you must also be self-motivated. As I write this, I'm filming *Drag Race*, recording an album, and developing several other film and TV projects. Exhausted? Damn right, I'm exhausted! But there's a reason I've been the top bitch in the game for more than twenty-five years. Remember, the best time to get a new job is when you already have one.

You're actually stronger than you allow yourself to be.

The bad news is that your inner saboteur never goes away. The good news is that it can be managed. I make peace with the destructive part of myself everyday that I live and breathe. I've learned to recognize the timbre of its voice. I know what it wants and how insidious it can be. Through much despair, I've learned that my best defense is to keep the playing field even, and maintain a balance by nurturing my higher Self. I get down on my knees and pray to disarm my Ego. When I physically kneel down to acknowledge a Higher Power, my Ego involuntarily submits. In truth, it really doesn't matter what you pray to. Just the act of doing it is enough for it to work. I also meditate by focusing on my breathing. That level of stillness creates open spaces in my consciousness for inspiration. I exercise, walk, bike, hike, dance, and eat food that is healthy and alive. All of these things counteract the heaviness of my saboteur, which wants to pull me down to the depths of despair and helplessness. I hear the voice of my darkness, and I say thanks for sharing, lover, but I'm going to do the opposite of what you're saying.

YOU OVERCOME THE "DARK NIGHT OF THE SOUL" BY PERSEVERING.

#LOOKBUTDONTSTARE

I always straighten up the house before our house-keeper comes. I want to put things away in a place where I can find them again. If I'm in a hotel, I don't want the person cleaning up after me to find a mess. If I'm in a limo, I will tell the driver that I'll get my own door. It's important for me to be self-sufficient. Twenty years ago, my therapist suggested that this

Willingly release the hurt. Don't let the heartache define you.

was because I have an issue with being beholden. She was right, I don't want to be obligated to any-one. I'd rather just do for myself. And she told me that the gift you can give to other people is allow-ing them to give *you* something. That blew my mind. Wow! That was a game changer.

Transformation, adaptability, alchemy, and the re-creating of self are the words I live by. Birth and death and rebirth are constant themes in life. Staying flexible, both figuratively and literally, is what being vital is all about. Seeing myself from outside of myself helps. My morning meditation helps with that. We are all constantly changing, but few are willing to embrace those changes. The crucifixion at the end of the first act is meaningless without the resurrection in the second act.

When the going gets tough, the tough reinvent themselves.

Humans are the only species who will deny their animal nature. We are animals and we are sexual beings. We have the ability to reproduce at puberty, yet we keep young people from the information they need to make wise sexual decisions. Knowledge is power. Defend your children by giving them the power of knowledge.

TO UNDERSTAND HUMANS, YOU MUST STUDY THEM AS A SPECIES OF ANIMAL.

I was taught to always make a good first impression because you'll never get a second chance. It all starts with the handshake. Anytime someone shakes my hand and does it half-heartedly, I correct them. By correcting them I'm saying you may not be engaged, but I certainly am.

A weak handshake coupled with no eye contact says the person is not present, not engaged, and not trustworthy.

Money is a means to get things done, but if you don't evolve your relationship to abundance, you will always be poor. That's why you hear about lottery winners who are broke five years later, because their relationship to abundance hasn't been

Some people are so poor, all they have is money.

remapped. A lot of people believe they don't deserve abundance, and the funny thing about abundance is that the more you have, the more you get. It's the law of attraction. And most people don't understand that concept.

Life is hard. There is no way to sugarcoat that cold, hard fact. Modern parents who've been extensively self-analyzed have taken it upon themselves to right the perceived wrongs of their childhood by making the world "baby-safe" for their children. That usually results in churning out a bunch of entitled little snot-nose brats who have no concept of truth or consequence. It's much more difficult to be the diligent voice thinking critically for your child. Children need boundaries. They want boundaries. I believe what keeps this dialogue from happening is the parent's own narcissism. Imagine a world where children are taught real processing tools, and where people wouldn't have the need to visit their internal struggle on other people. Handle your shit, ladykins!

The struggle is real, henny.

Peek-a-Ru,

I See U.

I like to press the proverbial Google Earth button from time to time to instantly change my perspective when shit done got too heavy. I will press that button to refresh my emotional state so I can see the whole landscape and go, "Oh, I'm focused on this one small thing over here? The truth is, that's not that important." Having that Google Earth button any time you feel flustered is always a great way to "refresh."

QUICK REMINDER:

Don't take life too seriously.

Sometimes I reboot my emotional system by listening to songs that make me cry real hard.

When you find success, sometimes you have to leave old friends behind. And sometimes you have to leave family members behind. It's sad and heartbreaking, but it must be done. You cannot bring everybody with you, because some will resent you and drag you down to a level that makes them feel more comfortable. Whether your success is money, fame, or weight loss, keep an eye out for people who feel threatened by your ascension. If they can evolve, there's a place for them. If not, then goodbye. Ever hear the phrase "It's lonely at the top"?

Ultimately, the fight for success is a battle with yourself.

I love dancing. I have always loved to dance. It's the way the human spirit gets aroused. The beat of dance music emulates the heartbeat, and we intuitively move to it and get lost in it, and losing yourself opens you up to greater possibilities. I'm so disappointed in these modern times that there aren't enough places to dance. I'd rather boogie than try to fit in. If other people can't get with the boogie, I have no time for them.

METAPHOR: THERE IS NO FREE LUNCH. YOU'LL PAY AT THE BEGINNING OF THE MEAL OR AT THE END, BUT TRUST ME, YOU WILL PAY.

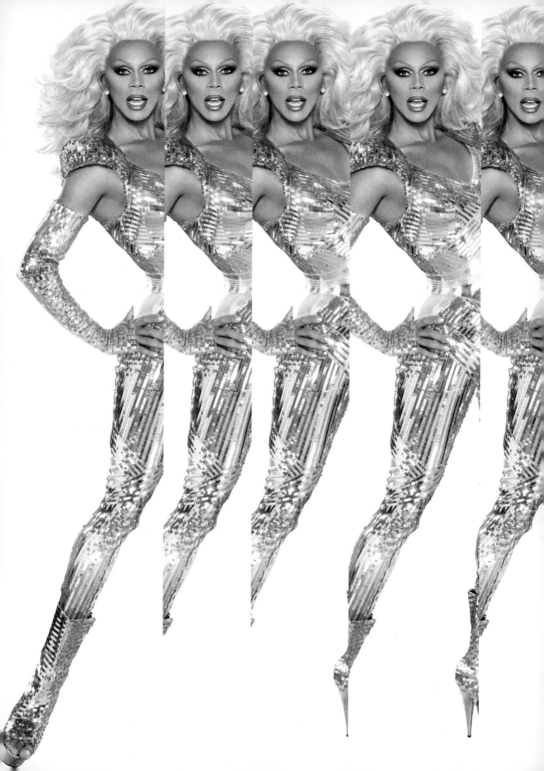

Shine, baby, shine for you. It is about self-preservation. It is the law of nature. It is about investing time in yourself and making sure you have enough love, that you've allotted love for yourself by taking the time to be kind to yourself and having some gratitude for this beautiful gift you've been given that is life. Being kind to myself is my gift to the world.

If you can't love yourself, how in the hell you gonna love somebody else?

I feel at my core that I am a teacher. I am here to be a

conduit. I know how to make magic. I have the ability to

help people cross over to their greatness and realize

their potential. My presence in the pop landscape has

Ego loves identity.
Drag mocks identity.
Ego hates drag.

allowed people to see themselves as their superhero.

Drag for me has always been my superhero costume. I

feel powerful in drag. I think other people see that and

believe they can do the same thing.

Painting the house won't fix a shaky foundation. Your foundation must be built on something solid, and that solid foundation is love—not the romantic rom-com, fairy tale love, but the frequency that runs through and connects each of us. You must clear a path within yourself for that frequency to live in you and so that your body can communicate that to the world. That is your job.

Ultimately, it's about the love you give and the love you allow yourself to receive. Everything else fades away.

I never set out to become a role model or a trailblazer. My mission was simply to explore life and clear a path within myself to allow the frequency to move through me. Busting through fear has been a constant challenge. Finding places in my consciousness where I feel stuck or unwilling to change is a real downer, but not insurmountable. I can also learn from the experience of others. I've learned a lot about life from the mistakes of people I admire. Strangely, that first relationship with my parents is still a touchstone for heartbreak. I know that's true for most people.

The ego perceives us as separate from one another, but we are not. We are one thing.

Now it can be told!

I am so proud of DragCon. People from all over the world who love *Drag Race* can communicate on social media, but there is nothing like meeting your tribe in person. Something magical happens in your consciousness on an emotional, visceral level that is undeniable. DragCon facilitates a conversation between the past and the future. There is no guidebook for the seeker on the road less traveled, but DragCon is a good place to start. It's a celebration of the tenacity of the human spirit.

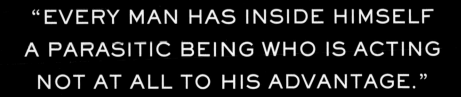

"EVERY MAN HAS INSIDE HIMSELF
A PARASITIC BEING WHO IS ACTING
NOT AT ALL TO HIS ADVANTAGE."
—WILLIAM S. BURROUGHS

I realize that no one has been crueler to me than I have been to myself. The most dangerous place on earth is inside my head. I laugh because otherwise I would cry. I have to give myself a break. This is also true for people who are unkind to other people—you have to realize that the unkindness that those people are projecting outwardly at innocent people is just a fraction of what they're doing to themselves.

How much are you willing to leave behind in order to lighten your load?

EMOTIONALLY WE
ARE STILL A VERY
PRIMITIVE CULTURE.

I have love for all the sweet sensitive souls. We transcend all labels, descriptions, and limitations. We are everything and nothing at all.

Your soul is made of stars.

We are all stars.

become your own guru

RUPAUL'S CURATED LIST OF MUST WATCH, READ, AND LISTEN-TOS

MUST-SEE FILMS

The Wizard of Oz

Grease

Mommie Dearest

Elvira: Mistress of the Dark

Paris Is Burning

The Rocky Horror Picture Show

Auntie Mame

The Matrix

Mahogany

Who's Afraid of Virginia Woolf?

Death Becomes Her

Network

Inception

Airplane!

What's Up, Doc?

Young Frankenstein

Two Can Play That Game

Sunset Boulevard

The Exorcist

Arthur

Funny Face

A Star Is Born (starring Judy Garland)

Sullivan's Travels

MUST-READ BOOKS

A Return to Love
by Marianne Williamson

Toxic Parents
by Dr. Susan Forward

The Velvet Rage
by Alan Downs

A New Earth
by Eckhart Tolle

My Life So Far
by Jane Fonda

Magical Thinking
by Augusten Burroughs

Me Talk Pretty One Day
by David Sedaris

MUST-HEAR ALBUMS

Stephanie Mills,
For the First Time
(written and produced by Burt
Bacharach and Hal David)

Alexandra Burke,
Heartbreak on Hold

Tina Turner,
Foreign Affair

Carly Simon,
No Secrets

Pointer Sisters,
Break Out

Grace Jones,
Slave to the Rhythm

David Bowie,
Station to Station

David Bowie,
Low

Britney Spears,
Femme Fatale

Britney Spears,
Glory

Natalie Cole,
Unforgettable: With Love

Whitney Houston,
My Love Is Your Love

Blondie,
Eat to the Beat

Giorgio Moroder,
American Gigolo soundtrack

Donna Summer,
Another Place and Time

Donna Summer,
Bad Girls

Kylie Minogue,
Aphrodite

Stevie Wonder,
Fulfillingness' First Finale

Bryan Ferry,
Bête Noire

Michael McDonald,
If That's What It Takes

Liza Minnelli
(with Pet Shop Boys),
Results

Diana Ross,
Everything Is Everything

Diana Ross,
The Boss

Elvis Costello
and Burt Bacharach,
Painted from Memory

Kiesza,
Sound of a Woman

Taylor Dayne,
Satisfied

*Dr. Buzzard's
Original Savannah Band*

Corona,
The Rhythm of the Night

Amber,
This Is My Night

Stevie Wonder,
Hotter Than July

Bonnie Raitt,
Nick of Time

Dusty Springfield,
A Brand New Me

Steely Dan,
Aja

Cher,
It's a Man's World

Booty Luv,
Boogie 2Nite

Regina Belle,
Reachin' Back

Nancy Wilson,
With My Lover Beside Me
(produced by Barry Manilow)

Kenny Rogers,
Eyes That See in the Dark
(written and produced
by the Bee Gees)

Dionne Warwick,
Heartbreaker
(written and produced
by the Bee Gees)

Barbra Streisand,
Guilty
(written and produced
by the Bee Gees)

Miles Davis,
Kind of Blue

Anita O'Day,
In a Mellow Tone

acknowledgments

It takes a village to get ready for the stage, and creating a book is a similar process. So, to my book glam squad, Thank You! First of all, to my editor, Carrie Thornton—I loved our conversations and how you "got" this book and what I wanted it to be. To Suet Chong, interior designer—you are so creative and talented! What a good eye you have. Ploy Siripant, thank you for this arresting cover. I know it is going to get people's attention. To the rest of the Dey Street Team, including Lynn Grady, Ben Steinberg, Heidi Richter, Julie Paulauski, Jessica Lyons, Andrea Molitor, and Sean Newcott.

Thank you to my right arm, Joelle Hawkes, Mathu Andersen, Zaldy, Randy Barbato, Thairin Smothers, Cait Hoyt, and all those on team RuPaul who keep the balls up in the air (and there are a lot of balls, henny!).

And always, love and thanks to the love of my life, Georges LeBar.

about the author

RuPaul produces and hosts the reality competition series *RuPaul's Drag Race*, for which he received two Primetime Emmy Awards in 2016 and 2017. He also hosts the podcast *RuPaul: What's the Tee?* with Michelle Visage.